# WHATEVER

**A Simple Strategy to Gain Clarity on Your Next Career Move.**

**Clayton Poland**

Copyright © 2023 Clayton Poland
All rights reserved. No part of this publication may be reproduced, distributed, or transmitted in any form or by any means, including photocopying, recording, or other electronic or mechanical methods, without the prior written permission of the publisher, except in the case of brief quotations embodied in reviews and certain other non-commercial uses permitted by copyright law.

Some names and details were changed to protect the privacy of the individuals in each story.

ISBN 9798862100563

# Dedication

To the seeker of wisdom, the explorer of change, and the courageous soul embarking on a transformative journey - may these pages illuminate your path, inspire your choices, and empower your evolution.

This book is dedicated to you, the intrepid traveler of life's uncharted territories.

# Contents

**Whatever**
The Mindset — 1

**Whoever**
Finding Your Tribe — 5

**However**
Discovering Your Preferred Workstyle — 11

**Whenever**
Understanding Flow in Your Work Life — 19

**Wherever**
Finding Your Ideal Work Environment — 25

**Whyever**
Finding Purpose in Your Workplace — 31

**Never, Ever, Whatsoever**
Unveiling Your Non-Negotiables in Work — 37

**Forever**
Embracing the Journey of Your Next Best Move — 43

**Whatever!**
Embracing Your Choice — 49

**The Evers**
The Journey Ahead — 57

Resources — 63
Notes — 73
About the Author — 83

CONTENTS

# WHATEVER
## The Mindset

***Whatever*** *you do, work at it with all your heart, as working for the Lord, not for human masters.*
Colossians 3:23 (NIV)

In a world filled with diverse beliefs, philosophies, and life paths, it's essential to acknowledge that wisdom can be found in unexpected places. Colossians 3:23 in the Bible encourages us to "***Whatever*** we do, do it with all our hearts as if we were serving the Lord." The question then becomes, "What does God want each of us to do with our lives...whatever!" Yet, regardless of our religious beliefs or spiritual inclinations, there's an undeniable truth that transcends faith – a "whatever" mindset can transform our professional lives.

It's important to clarify that the "Whatever" mindset is not an endorsement of every profession under the sun. We're not suggesting careers that are illegal, cause harm to others, or compromise our moral values. Instead, this book is a compass guiding us toward careers that align with our principles, values, and aspirations, be they in college, the skilled trades, the military, or any noble pursuit that resonates with our authentic selves.

Many of us have grown up in cultures or environments that emphasize finding a singular, well-defined path for our careers. However, the reality is starkly different. Statistics reveal that a staggering 85% of people are dissatisfied with their jobs, while less than 30% of college graduates find themselves working inside their field of study.

The seeds of change are sown when we recognize that we need a new approach to career decision-making, one that transcends the boundaries of tradition and ushers in a fresh perspective. This book is intentionally designed to be simple and straightforward, a practical guide for anyone seeking fulfillment and purpose in their professional journey.

The journey ahead may be simple, but it's far from easy. It requires a potent combination of honesty, self-reflection, and grit. Yet, the rewards are immeasurable. As we begin this transformative odyssey, we'll explore a framework built around eight profound words, each representing a chapter in this book.

These "Evers" will illuminate our path forward:
- **Whoever**: Finding Your Tribe
- **However**: Discovering Your Preferred Workstyle
- **Whenever**: Understanding Flow in Your Work
- **Wherever**: Finding Your Ideal Work Environment
- **Whyever**: Finding Purpose in Your Workplace
- **Never Ever Whatsoever**: Your Non-Negotiables
- **Forever**: Your Decisions Aren't Eternal
- **Whatever**: Embracing Your Career Choice

In the chapters that follow, we'll delve into each of these "Evers," uncovering the wisdom and insights they hold for our professional lives. Regardless of your background, beliefs, or experiences, I invite you to embark on this journey with an open heart and an inquisitive mind. The "Whatever" mindset knows no boundaries – it's a universal call to action, a beacon of hope, and a path toward a career that resonates with your soul.

Are you ready to explore the "Whatever" mindset in your professional life?

Your adventure begins now!

# WHATEVER

# WHOEVER

Finding Your Tribe

*Your direct supervisor has more effect on your health than your primary doctor.*
The Mayo Clinic

Life is all about relationships! Whether you consider yourself a people person or not, the reality of life is this, you have to engage with people in personal and professional settings each day. You get to choose who you work with each and every day. Gone are the days of working for a lifetime with and for people who don't value you as an individual. Given these realities, let's make the most of our relationships, especially our professional relationships.

The significance of professional relationships cannot be overstated, as they extend beyond the boundaries of the workplace and profoundly impact our overall well-being. An illuminating statistic from the Mayo Clinic underscores this point: your direct supervisor has a more influence on your health than your primary care physician. This relational dynamic underscores the interconnectedness of our work lives with our physical and mental health. A positive working relationship with your "work family" can reduce stress, enhance job satisfaction, and contribute to a healthier, more fulfilling life.

Our professional journeys are not solitary endeavors but rather collaborative symphonies. In the "Whoever" chapter, we celebrate the individuals who cross our paths, influence our choices, and shape our careers. "Whoever" encompasses not only the people we work alongside but also the mentors, partners, and allies who guide and inspire us. They are the architects of our growth, the catalysts of our success, and sometimes even the mirrors reflecting our true potential. As we embark on the transformative journey of professional change, let us embrace the profound impact of "Whoever" on our path, and let their wisdom and support illuminate our way forward.

Let's embark on this enlightening exploration into the realm of "Who" you enjoy doing life with and choose to work with. Below, you'll find journal-style questions to help you reflect on the people who have influenced and continue to influence your career choices.

## Whoever Reflection Questions:
1. Who are the individuals you naturally gravitate towards in social settings, and what qualities or characteristics do they share?

2. When you think about your closest friends, what common interests or values do you share with them?

3. Are there specific groups or communities you feel a strong sense of belonging to? What draws you to these groups?

4. Consider the people who encourage your personal and professional growth. Who are they, and what role do they play in your life?

5. In your work environment, who are the colleagues or team members you collaborate seamlessly with to achieve goals?

6. What is the communication style that makes you feel understood and valued by others, and who are the people that employ this style?

7. Imagine the future version of yourself in your desired career. What role do your "Whoever" individuals play in your vision of success, and how will you express your gratitude to them?

# WHATEVER

# HOWEVER

Discovering Your Preferred Workstyle

*How you do anything, is how you do everything.*
Martha Beck

Life and career choices are not one-size-fits-all; they are as unique as our fingerprints. The "However" chapter celebrates the diversity of paths we can take to reach our professional destinations. It reminds us that there is no single right way to achieve our goals and that embracing our individuality and uniqueness is a powerful catalyst for success. In "However," we explore the various methods, approaches, and styles that define our personal and professional journeys. As we consider our professional life, let's embrace the liberating power of "However" and acknowledge that the unconventional, the unexpected, and the unique can be our greatest assets.

Now, let's delve into the world of "However". Below, you'll find a few questions to help you reflect on your unique approach to work and life.

**However Reflection Questions:**
Questions to help you explore your preferences regarding how you like to work and live within organizational and leadership cultures:

**Work Preferences:**
1. What type of work environment motivates you the most: collaborative, competitive, individual-focused, or more of a balanced approach?

2. Are you more productive in structured or flexible work settings, and why?

3. What tools and technologies do you find most effective for enhancing your productivity and efficiency?

4. What work hours align best with your productivity and work-life balance needs? Are you comfortable with multitasking, or do you prefer to focus on one task at a time to maintain quality and concentration?

5. Are you more comfortable with remote work, on-site work, or a hybrid approach?

6. Do you thrive in organizations that emphasize innovation, stability, or a balance of both?

7. What role does a company's mission and values play in your work satisfaction?

8. How do you respond to company cultures that prioritize employee well-being and work-life balance?

9. Are you more motivated by financial rewards, career advancement, or personal growth opportunities?

10. Do you prefer organizations with hierarchical leadership structures or those that emphasize flat hierarchies and employee empowerment?

**Leadership Preferences:**
1. What leadership style resonates with you the most: authoritative, collaborative, transformational, or servant leadership?

2. How do you prefer to communicate with your superiors and leaders: open-door policy, regular one-on-one meetings, or team-based discussions?

3. How do you prefer to receive feedback and recognition for your work achievements?

4. Are you inspired by leaders who prioritize mentorship and employee development?

5. How important is transparency and honesty in leadership communication for you?

6. What approach to decision-making do you find most effective in leadership: data-driven, consensus-based, or visionary leadership?

7. Do you prefer leaders who are hands-on or those who trust their teams to work independently?

8. Are you more comfortable with leaders who lead by example or those who provide guidance and support from behind the scenes?

9. What role does ethical leadership and social responsibility play in your admiration for a leader?

10. How do you react to leaders who encourage and celebrate diversity, equity, and inclusion within their organizations?

## Your Ideal Workday

Considering your work and leadership preferences, reflect on your ideal workday. What elements would it include, and how can you align your current or future work habits with this vision?

WHATEVER

# WHENEVER

Understanding Flow in Your Work Life

*Success is the ability to go from one failure to the next without the loss of enthusiasm.*
Winston Churchill

The concept of "Whenever" invites us to explore the rhythms of our own productivity and creativity. It acknowledges that each of us has a unique internal clock, a time when we are most in sync with our tasks, and a time when we are in the flow of our best work. In this chapter, we delve into the art of timing, recognizing that the key to peak performance lies in understanding our individual "whenever." Whether it's the early hours of dawn, the tranquility of the afternoon, or the stillness of night, there's a "whenever" that resonates with your most productive and creative self. As you embark on your career change journey, let's discover the optimal "whenever" for your success.

Now, here are ten journal-style questions to guide your exploration of "Whenever" and when you do your best work:

**Whenever Reflection Questions:**
1. Reflect on your daily routine. At what times of day do you typically feel most energized and focused? Describe the characteristics of these moments.

2. Think about your past accomplishments. Can you recall instances when you were "in the zone" or experienced a state of flow? What were the circumstances and time of day?

3. Consider your work environment. Are there specific times when you find it easier to concentrate and be productive due to external factors, such as reduced noise or distractions?

4. Reflect on your natural circadian rhythms. Do you have a preference for morning, afternoon, or evening activities? How can you align your tasks with these rhythms for optimal performance?

5. Explore your creative processes. Are there certain times when you feel more inspired and imaginative? How can you leverage these moments in your career change journey?

6. Think about deadlines and time management. How can you schedule your tasks and goals to align with your most productive "whenever" hours?

7. Consider your current work schedule. Does it accommodate your ideal "whenever" times, or are there adjustments you can make to optimize your productivity?

8. Reflect on your ability to recharge and rest. How do breaks and downtime factor into your workday, and how can they contribute to maintaining your peak performance?

9. Consider the role of flexibility. How open are you to adjusting your schedule and routine to accommodate your optimal "whenever" hours during your career change?

# WHENEVER

# WHATEVER

# WHEREVER

Finding Your Ideal Work Environment

*Home is not where you live but where they understand you.*
Christian Morgenstern

Our careers are not bound by geographic constraints; they are as limitless as our aspirations. The "Wherever" chapter encourages us to explore the vast possibilities of where we can build our professional lives. It invites us to consider that our dream job might not just be around the corner but across borders, in different cities, or in places we've yet to discover. The "Wherever" celebrates the freedom to choose our workplace and environment, reminding us that location can be a powerful source of inspiration and growth. As we embark on the journey of career change, let us embrace the boundless potential of "Wherever" and open our hearts to the idea that our dream job might be waiting in a place we've never imagined.

Now, let's dive into the world of "Wherever" in your career change journey. Below, you'll find journal-style questions to help you reflect on the locations and environments that resonate with your professional aspirations.

**Wherever Reflection Questions:**
1. What type of climate and weather do you prefer in your ideal location?

2. Do you prefer to work inside, outside, or a mixture of both.

3. Do you prefer a bustling city, a quiet town, or a remote countryside to live and work?

4. What regions or countries have always intrigued you, and why?

5. Do you prioritize proximity to family and friends when choosing a place to live and work?

6. What lifestyle do you envision for yourself in your ideal location?

7. Are there specific cultural aspects or values you'd like your chosen location to align with?

8. How do career opportunities and industries in different regions influence your choice?

9. Are you open to relocating for work, and if so, what factors would motivate you to make such a move?

10. How important is access to outdoor activities, parks, or nature in your decision?

11. Are there historical landmarks, cultural events, or attractions you'd like to be close to?

12. Does your ideal location require proximity to specific amenities, such as schools, healthcare facilities, or shopping centers?

13. Are you willing to learn a new language or adapt to a different culture if it enhances your chosen location?

14. Are you open to frequent travel for work, and how might this impact your choice of location?

15. Do you have any preferences for the cost of living, and how does it align with potential locations?

16. What compromises are you willing to make, and what are your non-negotiables when choosing where to live and work?

17. Have you sought advice or insights from people who have experience living and working in different locations?

WHATEVER

# WHYEVER

Finding Purpose in Your Workplace

*It is the glory of God to conceal a matter;
to search out a matter is the glory of kings.*
Proverbs 25:2 NIV

In the grand tapestry of our professional lives, the "Whyever" chapter guides us to unravel the threads of purpose woven into our chosen organizations. It reminds us that our careers are not just about earning a paycheck but about contributing to a larger mission, a deeper "why" that aligns with our values and beliefs.

"Whyever" celebrates the importance of finding meaning and purpose in the organizations we choose to work for. As we navigate our career path, let's explore how our unique passions and values can be harnessed to create a profound impact in our chosen fields. The "Whyever" chapter encourages us to ask not only "Why am I changing my career?" but also "Why am I choosing this organization, and how does it resonate with my sense of purpose?"

Now, let's immerse ourselves in the "Whyever" concept in your career change journey. Below, you'll find several questions to help you reflect on the deeper purpose and mission of the organizations you aspire to join.

**Whyever Reflection Questions:**
1. Consider your personal values and beliefs. What causes or missions align with your core principles, and how can you incorporate them into your career change? (Refer to the Resource section for a list of values to consider.)

2. Reflect on your past experiences. Have you ever been part of an organization with a mission that deeply resonated with you? What made that experience meaningful?

3. Think about your current understanding of the organizations in your desired career field. Are there specific organizations whose mission statements or values align with your sense of purpose?

4. Explore the impact you want to make through your career. How does the mission and purpose of an organization contribute to your ability to create positive change in the world?

5. Consider your potential role within an organization. How can your unique skills and passions contribute to the organization's mission and goals?

6. Reflect on the ethical and moral standards of the organizations you're considering. Are there any organizations whose values or practices are non-negotiable for you?

7. Think about the role of corporate social responsibility and sustainability in your career change. How important is it for the organization to align with your values in these areas?

8. Consider your willingness to advocate for causes you believe in within your chosen organization. How can you leverage your position to promote positive change?

9. Reflect on the alignment between your personal sense of purpose and the organization's overarching mission. How can these elements harmoniously coexist in your career?

10. Imagine yourself thriving in your new career within an organization that embodies your values. How does the alignment of purpose contribute to your sense of fulfillment and success in this role?

# WHATEVER

# NEVER, EVER, WHATSOEVER

Unveiling Your Non-Negotiables in Work and Life

*My values are non-negotiable. And if it means not getting a role, it means not getting a role.*
Cassidy Erin Gifford

In the grand tapestry of our professional lives, there exist certain threads that should never be compromised - our core values, our deeply held beliefs, and the unwavering boundaries that define who we are and what we stand for. The "Never Ever Whatsoever" chapter is a sanctuary for those principles that are non-negotiable, a space where we assert, "I will never, ever, whatsoever, go against these guiding lights."

As we navigate the complexities of our career and self-discovery, let's not forget the importance of staying true to ourselves. This chapter invites you to reflect on those unyielding convictions, to cherish them as the compass guiding you toward the professional path that truly aligns with your essence.

Now, let's delve into introspection and explore the boundaries you've set for your career journey. Below, you'll find some questions to help you articulate and reinforce the "Never Ever Whatsoever" principles and boundaries that define your professional identity.

**Never, Ever, Whatsoever Reflection Questions:**
1. What are the core values that you hold dear in your professional journey, and which ones are non-negotiable under any circumstances? (Refer to the Resource section for a list of values to consider.)

2. Reflect on past experiences. Can you recall a time when you compromised on a principle or value in your career? How did it make you feel, and what did you learn from that experience?

3. Are there specific ethical or moral standards that you will never, ever, whatsoever compromise on in your professional life? What makes these principles so significant to you?

4. Think about work-related boundaries. What are the boundaries you've set for your work-life balance, and how will you ensure they are respected in your future career?

5. Are there certain types of tasks, projects, or roles that you will never accept, no matter how tempting they may be? What drives this decision?

6. Consider your interpersonal relationships at work. What behaviors or actions from colleagues or superiors will you never tolerate, and why?

7. Reflect on the impact you want to make through your career. What positive change or contribution do you want to bring to the world, and what compromises will you never make in pursuit of this mission?

8. What personal well-being practices or self-care routines will you always prioritize, regardless of your professional commitments? How will you maintain this balance?

## NEVER, EVER, WHATSOEVER

9. Are there specific industries, sectors, or organizations that you will never, ever, whatsoever associate with due to their values or practices? What motivates this stance?

10. Imagine your ideal professional journey. How will staying true to your "Never, Ever, Whatsoever" principles empower you to create a fulfilling and authentic career path?

# WHATEVER

# FOREVER

Embracing the Journey of Your Next Best Move

*Your life is a result of the choices you've made.
Don't like your life, start making better choices.*
Zig Ziglar

In the grand narrative of our careers, the "Forever" chapter reminds us that our choices are not etched in stone but written in the fluid ink of possibility. It invites us to embrace the idea that a career change is not necessarily a permanent decision but a meaningful stepping stone on our professional journey.

The "Forever" mindset celebrates the freedom to explore, evolve, and adapt, understanding that the only constant is change itself. As we embark on our professional career, let us release the weight of permanence and instead carry the lightness of forever - a forever filled with growth, learning, and endless opportunities.

Now, let's dive into the "Forever" concept. Below, you'll find questions to help you reflect on the idea that your choices are not set in stone and that there is always room for evolution.

**Forever Reflection Questions:**
1. Reflect on your current perspective. How do you view your career choice - is it a permanent commitment or a step on a larger journey?

2. Consider your long-term career aspirations. How does this career choice align with your broader professional goals and the potential for future evolution?

3. Explore the concept of adaptability. How open are you to adjusting your career path as you gain new experiences and insights in your chosen field?

4. Reflect on your personal growth and development. How does the idea of a "forever" journey influence your commitment to continuous learning and self-improvement?

5. Think about the role of flexibility in your career change strategy. How can you remain open to unexpected opportunities and changes in direction?

6. Consider the impact of change on your work-life balance. How can you maintain equilibrium as your career evolves over time?

7. Consider the impact of industry innovation on your career choices. How does having a "forever" mindset influence your commitment to continuous learning and self-improvement?

8. Explore the concept of resilience. How can you build resilience to navigate the challenges and uncertainties that may arise on your career journey?

# FOREVER

# WHATEVER

# WHATEVER!

## Embracing Your Choice

*Whatever you do, work at it with all your heart, as working for the Lord, not for human masters.*
Colossians 3:23 (NIV)

As we embark on this closing chapter of our journey together, we find ourselves at a pivotal moment - a moment where we stand poised to embrace the profound power of the "Whatever" mindset as it relates to our career. This chapter represents the culmination of our exploration into the facets of work and life, into the "How," "When," "Where," "Who," and "Why" that shape our professional destinies.

Throughout our voyage, we've done a deep dive into the intricacies of how we work, when we do our best work, where we choose to work, who we work with, and why we are drawn to certain organizations. Each of these dimensions has illuminated our path, offering insights, revelations, and newfound clarity.

But now, it's time to bring it all together. It's time to celebrate the magnificent tapestry of choices and discoveries we've made. It's time to say, "Whatever we choose, we will go after it with all our heart, soul, mind, and strength."

Amidst the vast array of career possibilities, the "Whatever" mindset beckons us to become intentional architects of our professional destinies. It reminds us that, in a world of endless options, the power to choose is a precious gift. "Whatever" celebrates the art of discernment, guiding us to sift through the myriad opportunities and focus on what truly resonates. It encourages us to let go of the "what-ifs" and instead embrace the "what matters most."

This is where the rubber meets the road for your career journey. The Whatever mindset is about reflecting on the work we've done thus far, then narrowing down our endless career options into three possible paths that we can evaluate.

## Narrowing Down Your Career Choices

**Career Choice 1:** _____

In this scenario, everything works out. You love the position, the organization, the leadership, the scope of work, your coworkers, your title, etc. You find this career choice exhilarating and challenging. You're excited to learn everything you can so you can advance in this industry.

**Career Choice 2:** _____

For whatever reason(s), Career Choice 1 doesn't work out. You don't like the organization, the position, the scope of work, the title, the leadership, your coworkers, etc. Maybe the content doesn't come as naturally to you as you'd hoped for. Since Career Choice 1 didn't work out, you're excited to explore Career Choice 2.

**Career Choice 3:** _____

This is the wild card option. The "I've always wondered..." option. Or as I sometimes say to audiences, this is the "I've always wondered what it would be like to run a tiki hut on the beach." For whatever reasons, Career Choices 1 and 2 didn't work out. This is a good thing! It doesn't mean you're a failure, it means you've found two career paths that aren't right for you at this time.

# WHATEVER!

Now, considering these three career choices, let's dive into some "Whichever" questions to help ensure these choices align with your values and aspirations. It is absolutely essential that you be honest with yourself! If you find yourself struggling in this section, enlist the help of a trusted friend or mentor.

**Whatever Reflection Questions:**
1. Reflect on your three career choices. What resonates most with you about each one?

2. Consider your core values and beliefs. How do these values influence your choices, and which career options align most closely with them?

3. Explore the concept of prioritization. What factors are most important to you in your career choice, and how can you rank them to clarify your focus?

4. Reflect on your skills and strengths. Do these three career options allow you to leverage your unique talents and experiences for success?

5. Think about the impact you want to make in your chosen field. Which career path enables you to contribute most effectively to your desired goals and outcomes?

6. Consider the role of passion and fulfillment. Do these career options ignite your passion and align with your sense of purpose?

7. Reflect on external factors such as market demand, opportunities for growth, and work-life balance. How do these factors impact each of your three career choices?

8. Think about your personal and professional support network. Who can provide guidance and insights to help you make informed choices regarding these three career choices?

9. Who do you personally know that's currently working in each of these three career fields? Set up a time to speak with them about what a day, week, month, or year actually looks like for this career.

10. YouTube is a great place to discover content creators who share their real-life experiences working in your chosen career field. What insights and lessons can you gather from their firsthand accounts, and how might this knowledge inform your career aspirations?

# WHATEVER!

# WHATEVER

# THE EVERS

The Journey Ahead

*Whatever you do, work at it with all your heart, as working for the Lord, not for human masters.*
Colossians 3:23 (NIV)

In closing, this book has been a journey of self-discovery, empowerment, and transformation. Through the exploration of life's "Evers" - Whatever, Wherever, Whenever, Whoever, However, and Whyever - you've embarked on a profound quest to define your career path, values, passions, and purpose. You've explored the depths of your own aspirations, and in doing so, you've laid the foundation for a career and life that aligns with your authentic self.

You've celebrated "Whoever," those individuals who inspire and uplift you, forming a network of support and mentorship to guide your journey.

You've unraveled the intricacies of "However," realizing that your approach to work is a reflection of your values and preferences, and that finding your unique way of operating is key to your success.

# WHATEVER

You've harnessed the magic of "Whenever," recognizing your own peak moments of productivity and creativity, and the importance of syncing your tasks with your internal clock.

You've discovered the power of "Wherever," understanding that your environment can shape your success, and that choosing the right place to work and thrive is a vital decision.

You've uncovered the profound "Whyever," understanding that your career isn't just about simply earning a paycheck - it's about contributing to a greater mission, a purpose that resonates with your heart and soul.

You've learned what you're "Never, Ever, Whatsoever" willing to compromise on in your life and career. Plus realized that this career choice isn't a "Forever" choice, but a well thought out decision that can be changed when circumstances beyond my control change.

Finally, you've learned that "Whatever" isn't about settling; it's about making intentional choices, embracing your uniqueness, and pursuing your dreams with unwavering determination.

Now, as you stand on the threshold of your new career, remember that this isn't the end; it's just the beginning. Armed with newfound clarity and a resilient spirit, you're ready to step boldly into your future. The "Whatever" mindset is your compass, your guiding star, and your unwavering belief that you can achieve your dreams.

Check out the resources in the back of the book. I've included a few fun and playful ways to explore your career. You'll also find lists of values for you to consider for your personal and professional life. Personal and professional values are the anchor for your soul, ensuring you navigate your life and career with alignment to your authentic self.

So, go forth with courage, passion, and a deep sense of purpose. Embrace the "Whatever" mindset in your life and career. Take action, avoid fear, and remember that your choice isn't an inescapable prison - it's your key to the door of possibility. Your journey is uniquely yours, and it's time to embark on the path that leads to the fulfillment, success, and happiness you deserve.

The "Whatever" mindset brought you the wisdom gained from your exploration. We understand that our choices are not merely decisions; they are commitments to a life lived with purpose, passion, and integrity. It's a commitment to embracing the "Whatever" mindset, knowing that we have the power to shape our lives.

I believe in you my friend!

WHATEVER

# WHATEVER!

# RESOURCES

# RESOURCES

# RESOURCES

# Personal Values

| | | |
|---|---|---|
| Integrity | Love | Health and wellness |
| Honesty | Generosity | Continuous learning |
| Respect | Tolerance | Freedom |
| Compassion | Open-mindedness | Innovation |
| Empathy | Perseverance | Justice |
| Accountability | Optimism | Teamwork |
| Transparency | Courage | Self-discipline |
| Authenticity | Independence | Excellence |
| Gratitude | Responsibility | Self-respect |
| Kindness | Flexibility | Self-awareness |
| Fairness | Creativity | Leadership |
| Loyalty | Curiosity | Achievement |
| Trustworthiness | Empowerment | Resilience |
| Patience | Family | Adventure |
| Humility | Community | Balance |
| Relationships | Growth | Harmony |

# Professional Workplace Values

| | | |
|---|---|---|
| Integrity | Flexibility | Initiative |
| Ethical Conduct | Problem-solving | Adaptability |
| Accountability | Communication | Time Management |
| Transparency | Empathy | Accountability |
| Professionalism | Continuous Improvement | Decision Making |
| Respect for others | Accountability | Goal Orientation |
| Trustworthiness | Vision | Research |
| Honesty | Enviro. Responsibility | Resilience |
| Excellence | Health and Safety | Patience |
| Quality | Sustainability | Results Driven |
| Customer Focus | Social Responsibility | Professional Growth |
| Innovation | Creativity | Independence |
| Collaboration | Customer Satisfaction | Knowledge Sharing |
| Teamwork | Efficiency | Positive attitude |
| Leadership | Reliability | Resourcefulness |
| Adaptability | Work-Life Balance | Ethical Leadership |

## A Professional Assessment:

1. What are your top three professional strengths or skills that you believe set you apart from others?
2. Reflecting on your work experiences, what have been the most fulfilling moments or projects, and what made them stand out to you?
3. What aspects of your current job or career bring you the most satisfaction and joy?
4. Consider your ideal work environment: What physical, cultural, or organizational attributes are essential for your productivity and happiness?
5. How do you prefer to collaborate with others: independently, in small teams, or in large group settings?
6. Are there specific times of day when you feel most productive and focused in your work?
7. What values and principles are non-negotiable for you in your professional life, and which ones are flexible?
8. Think about your long-term career goals: What are the key milestones you aspire to achieve?
9. How do you envision your work contributing to a larger purpose or making a positive impact in the world?
10. In what ways have you adapted and evolved in your professional journey so far, and how open are you to future changes and growth?

These questions can serve as a valuable self-assessment tool to reflect on your professional aspirations and preferences, helping you gain clarity on your path forward.

## Systems Over Goals

Scott Adams, the creator of the famous comic strip "Dilbert," introduced a compelling concept that has resonated with many in the realm of personal and professional development: "systems over goals." This idea challenges the conventional wisdom of setting specific, outcome-focused goals and instead advocates for the creation of sustainable systems or processes.

The value of the "systems over goals" concept lies in its adaptability and its ability to foster continuous progress. Here are several key reasons why this approach holds such importance:

**Focus on Process:** Goals often emphasize the end result, which can lead to a fixation on the destination rather than the journey. Systems, on the other hand, shift the focus to the daily actions and processes that, when consistently executed, move you closer to your objectives.

**Consistency:** Systems encourage consistency and regular effort, which is crucial for long-term success. While goals may be achieved and then forgotten, systems remain in place, providing a sustainable framework for ongoing growth.

**Adaptability:** Life is unpredictable, and circumstances change. Systems are more adaptable to unforeseen challenges, allowing you to adjust and pivot as needed while still progressing toward your aspirations.

**Less Pressure:** The pressure associated with achieving a specific goal can be overwhelming and discouraging. Systems reduce this pressure by emphasizing small, manageable steps, making the journey more enjoyable and less stressful.

**Continuous Improvement:** Systems are designed to foster continuous improvement. They encourage you to refine your processes, learn from mistakes, and iterate toward better outcomes over time.

**Long-Term Impact:** Goals often have a finite timeline, and once achieved, their impact can wane. Systems, however, are designed to create lasting habits and behaviors that can positively influence various aspects of your life indefinitely.

**Lifestyle Integration:** Systems can be integrated into your daily life more seamlessly than ambitious, one-time goals. They become a part of who you are, making it easier to maintain your progress over the long haul.

**Resilience:** Systems build resilience. When setbacks occur, you don't abandon your journey; instead, you adjust your system and keep moving forward.

In essence, the "systems over goals" concept reminds us that success is not merely a destination but a lifelong pursuit. It encourages us to focus on the journey, build sustainable habits, and navigate the ever-changing landscape of life with adaptability and resilience. As my friend Dr Bill Huggett suggests, "The journey is part of the gift." By prioritizing systems, individuals can unlock the true value of consistent progress, regardless of the specific objectives they choose to pursue.

## The Talent Stack

Another of Scott Adams contributions to the professional landscape journey is a concept known as the "talent stack." This idea challenges the conventional notion that success hinges solely on having a single, exceptional talent. Instead, Adams suggests that combining a modest set of skills can yield remarkable results. It's an exercise that encourages readers to reflect on their unique combination of abilities and how they can be leveraged to achieve their aspirations.

The essence of a talent stack lies in synergy. When you develop a range of competencies that complement each other, you create a powerful synergy that sets you apart from others. Consider the musician who pairs their musical talent with skills in marketing, creating a personal brand that propels their career. Or the software engineer who combines coding skills with effective communication, becoming a sought-after leader in their field.

Here's an exercise to explore your own talent stack:
**Self-Assessment:** Begin by assessing your existing skills and talents. What are you naturally good at? These might include artistic abilities, analytical thinking, communication skills, or physical fitness.

**Passions and Interests:** Identify your passions and interests. What activities or subjects captivate your attention and energize you? Your passions are often a source of motivation to develop related skills.

**Skill Development:** List the skills you've actively cultivated. These could be learned through education, practice, or self-study. Include both hard skills (e.g., programming, design, or financial analysis) and soft skills (e.g., leadership, communication, or creativity).

**Intersections:** Explore the intersections between your skills and interests. Where do your talents and passions overlap? These intersections represent unique opportunities to build a talent stack.

**Synergy:** Consider how combining these skills can create a synergistic effect. For example, if you have design skills and a passion for environmental sustainability, you might become a sustainable design advocate.

**Goal Alignment:** Evaluate how your talent stack aligns with your goals and aspirations. Does it open doors to the kind of career or impact you desire?

**Continuous Improvement:** Recognize that a talent stack is not static. It evolves as you acquire new skills and adapt to changing circumstances. Commit to lifelong learning and skill development.

Scott Adams' concept of a talent stack underscores the idea that your unique combination of skills and passions can set you on a path to success and fulfillment. By exploring your own talent stack, you can uncover hidden potential and identify opportunities to achieve your goals in a way that is uniquely yours.

See the following page for a brief list of professional skills. As you look over this list, which do you currently possess, and which do you wish to develop for your professional career?

# Useful Professional Skills

| | | |
|---|---|---|
| Graphic Design | Photography | Product Management |
| Coding/Programming | Search Engine Opt. (SEO) | Market Research |
| Data Analysis | Customer Service | Strategic Planning |
| Digital Marketing | Sales | Creativity |
| Project Management | Web Development | Adaptability |
| Writing | Content Creation | Problem Solving |
| Public Speaking | Presentation Skills | Social Media Marketing |
| Time Management | Research Skills | Video Production |
| Negotiation | Networking | 3D Printing |
| Financial Planning | Event Planning | Artificial Intelligence |
| Leadership | Team Collaboration | Blockchain Technology |
| Problem Solving | Emotional Intelligence | Virtual Reality |
| Critical Thinking | Conflict Resolution | Cybersecurity |
| Social Media Management | Public Relations | Cloud Computing |
| Foreign Language | Data Visualization | App Development |
| Video Editing | Branding | Content Strategy |

# WHATEVER

Use the following pages as your own career Whatever journal.

# NOTES

# NOTES

NOTES

# NOTES

# NOTES

# NOTES

## ABOUT THE AUTHOR

Clayton Poland is a civil engineer turned author, speaker, and storyteller who 's traveled nearly a million miles with his family encouraging folks to focus on the good stuff. For him, that most important good stuff is family.

He married his high school sweetheart Leigh and they have four amazing kids; Ethan, Maddie, Charlie, and Maria, their exchange student daughter from Guatemala. West Monroe, LA is their home and when he's not speaking and inspiring people across this great country, he can be found hanging out with family and friends enjoying good food and good conversation.

You can find out more about Clayton by visiting his website www.ClaytonPoland.com.

## ADDITIONAL RESOURCES

Clayton has several books, journals and resources to help you live life to the fullest. For more info, go to ClaytonPoland.com

Made in the USA
Columbia, SC
17 September 2024

c65d2356-b31e-4ae4-8f2d-525210d2bac1R02